VISIONS OF THE SPIRITUAL WORLD

A BRIEF DESCRIPTION OF THE SPIRITUAL REALM,
ITS DIFFERENT STATES OF EXISTENCE, AND THE
DESTINY OF GOOD AND EVIL MEN AS SEEN IN
VISIONS

BY SADHU SUNDAR SINGH

Originally published in 1926.

FOREWORD

I feel it a very great privilege to be allowed to accede to the request of my friend, Sadhu Sundar Singh, that I would write a brief foreword to his book "Visions", because I hope and believe that the little book will help many souls in their struggle to find Reality. I wish that all who read the book could have the privilege, that we in this Diocese and a number of people in London also have, of knowing the Sadhu personally. The message of the book gets an added force from the impression of a sweet sanity and simplicity that is left in one's mind after a talk with the Sadhu.

Inevitably, I think, some who read the book will feel impelled to ask the question: "What is the exact nature of these spiritual experiences? What, for instance, was the part played in them by the sub-conscious mind? Had what was seen in the 'Visions' an objective reality?"

I have not the philosophical knowledge that would enable me to give an answer to these questions: and I am by no means sure that, if I had it, I should feel that there would be any profit in using it in this case. S. Paul was content to leave his deepest spiritual experiences without full explanation. "Whether in the body or out of the body I cannot tell: God knoweth." The simplest view to my mind seems the truest. I read the book in Manuscript one Sunday afternoon in Simla this summer, and as I tried afterwards to analyse my impression, I felt it was this. I felt that for me the veil, which normally shrouds the real world, had been for a few moments lifted and that I had been allowed, through the help of Christ's faithful servant, to see things as they really are. I do not know, but I am inclined to think that my friend the Sadhu would himself prefer that the "visions" should be "explained" in this completely simple way. As I let my mind dwell on what I had read in the little book, a passage of Scripture came up over the margin of consciousness into my conscious mind, as recounting what was in some sense a parallel experience.

In all the conflicting opinions about the coming of the Kingdom of God, we have our Blessed Lord's own authority for its having come in one particular way. "There be some here that shall not taste of death till they have seen the Kingdom of God come with power." In both S. Mark's and S. Matthew's Gospels these words are so closely linked on to the story of the Transfiguration that I cannot doubt that they interpreted this memorable event in the life of the three chosen Disciples (one of whom was, as it were, the sponsor of S. Mark's Gospel) as a coming of the Kingdom with power. It consisted in the lifting of the veil which shrouds the unseen world, so that the denizens of that world were visible and audible to human eyes and ears, and in the glory of the real Jesus shining through the veil of flesh.

May it not be that this kind of experience is still given sometimes to God's servants? I personally believe that the Sadhu's experiences recounted in these "Visions" were something of this kind: that for him, as for these other servants of God, the veil which shrouds the real was lifted, so that he saw our Lord as He really is, and that world.

Messages that come as the result of such experiences must be reverenced, but they must also be tested by reference to the revelation of God in Jesus Christ. I have tried my best to apply this "test" to these messages, and I find them in accord with that supreme revelation of God's character which we have in our Lord's life and teaching. I therefore gratefully accept them as one more proof that God is still speaking to His people, and I pray that this little book may open the eyes of many to "the real world" that is all round us, to which we are too often blind, for "closer is He than breathing, and nearer than hands and feet".

H. B. LAHORE.

Simla,

6th August 1926.

PREFACE

In this book I have attempted to write about some of the visions which God has given me. Had I considered my own inclinations, I would not have published the account of these visions during my lifetime; but friends, whose judgment I value, have been insistent that, as a spiritual help to others, the publication of the teaching of these visions should not be delayed. In deference to the wish of these friends this book is now presented to the public.

At Kotgarh, fourteen years ago, while I was praying, my eyes were opened to the Heavenly Vision. So vividly did I see it all that I thought I must have died, and that my soul had passed into the glory of heaven; but throughout the intervening years these visions have continued to enrich my life. I cannot call them up at will, but, usually when I am praying or meditating, sometimes as often as eight or ten times in a month, my spiritual eyes are opened to see within the heavens, and, for an hour or two, I walk in the glory of the heavenly sphere with Christ Jesus, and hold converse with angels and spirits. Their answers to my questions have provided much of the material that has already been published in my books, and the unutterable ecstasy of that spiritual communion makes me long for the time when I shall enter in permanently to the bliss and fellowship of the redeemed.

Some may consider that these visions are merely a form of spiritualism, but I would emphasise that there is one very essential difference. Spiritualism does presume to produce messages and signs from spirits out of the dark, but they are usually so fragmentary and unintelligible, if not actually deceptive, that they lead their followers away from, rather than to, the truth. In these visions, on the other hand, I see vividly and clearly every detail of the glory of the spiritual world, and I have the uplifting experience of very real fellowship with the saints, amid the inconceivably bright and beautiful surroundings of a spiritual world made visible. It is from these angels and saints that I have received, not vague, broken and elusive messages from the unseen, but clear and rational elucidations of many of the problems that have troubled me.

This "Communion of the Saints" was a fact so real in the experience of the early Church, that it is given a place among the necessary articles of their faith, as stated in the "Apostles' Creed". Once, in a vision, I asked the saints for a proof from the Bible of this communion of saints, and was told that it was to be found clearly given in Zechariah iii. 7-8, where "those that were standing by" were not angels, nor "men" of flesh and blood, but saints in glory; and God's promise, on condition of Joshua fulfilling His command, is that he will be given "a place of access to walk among them (saints) that stand by", and these are his "fellows"—the spirits of men made perfect with whom he could commune.

There is repeated mention of Spirits, Saints and Angels in this book. The distinction I would make between them is that Spirits are both good and bad, who after death exist in a state intermediate between heaven and hell. Saints are those who have passed on through this stage into the higher sphere of the spiritual world, and have had special service allotted to them. Angels are those glorious beings to whom all kinds of superior service has been allotted, and among them are included many saints from other worlds, as well as from this world of ours, who all live together as one family. They serve one another in love, and, in the effulgence of God's glory, are eternally happy. The World of Spirits means that intermediate state into which spirits enter after leaving the body. By the Spiritual World is meant all spiritual beings that progress through the stages between the darkness of the bottomless pit and the throne of the Lord in light.

I wish to express my sincere thanks to the Rev. T. E. Riddle of the New Zealand Presbyterian Mission, Kharar, Punjab, who has journeyed up to Subathu to translate this book from Urdu into English. My thanks are again due to Miss E. Sanders, of Coventry, for having corrected the proofs of this book.

Sundar Singh.

Subathu, July, 1926.

CONTENTS:

CHAPTER I

LIFE AND DEATH

Life

There is only one source of Life—an Infinite and Almighty Life, Whose creative power gave life to all living things. All creatures live in Him, and in Him will they remain for ever. Again, this Life created innumerable other lives, different in kind, and in the stages of their progress man is one of these, created in God's own image that he might ever remain happy in His holy presence.

Death

This life may change but it can never be destroyed, and though the change from one form of existence into another is called Death, this never means that death finally ends life, or even that it adds to the life, or takes away anything from it. It merely transfers the life from one form of existence to another. A thing that disappears from our sight has not thereby ceased to exist. It reappears, but in another form and state. Man can never be destroyed

Nothing in this whole universe was ever destroyed, nor can it ever be, because the Creator has never created anything for destruction. If He had wished to destroy it, He would never have created it. And if nothing in creation can be destroyed, then how can man be destroyed, who is the crown of creation, and the image of his Creator? Can God Himself destroy His own image, or can any other creature do it? Never! If man is not destroyed at death, then at once the question rises, where will man exist after death, and in what state?

I shall attempt to give a brief explanation from my own visional experiences, though it is not possible for me to describe all the things which I have seen in visions of the spiritual world, because the language and illustrations of this world are inadequate to express these spiritual realities; and the very attempt to reduce to ordinary language the glory of the things seen is likely to result in misunderstanding. I have, therefore, had to eliminate the account of all those subtle spiritual occurrences, for which only a spiritual language is adequate, and to take up only a few simple and instructive incidents that will prove profitable to all. And since at some time or other every one will have to enter into this unseen spiritual world it will not be without profit if we, to some extent, become familiar with it.

CHAPTER II

WHAT HAPPENS AT DEATH?

One day when I was praying alone, I suddenly found myself surrounded by a great concourse of spirit beings, or I might say that as soon as my spiritual eyes were opened I found myself bowed in the presence of a considerable company of saints and angels. At first I was somewhat abashed, when I saw their bright and glorious state and compared with them my own inferior quality. But I was at once put at ease by their real sympathy and love-inspired friendliness. I had already had the experience of the peace of the presence of God in my life, but the fellowship with these saints added a new and wonderful joy to me. As we conversed together I received from them answers to my questions relating to my difficulties about many problems that puzzled me. My first inquiry was about what happens at the time of dying and about the state of the soul after death. I said, "We know what happens to us between childhood and old age, but we know nothing of what happens at the time of death or beyond the gates of death. Correct information about it can be known only by those on the other side of death, after they have entered the spiritual world. Can you", I asked, "give us any information about this?"

To this one of the saints answered, "Death is like sleep. There is no pain in the passing over, except in the case of a few bodily diseases and mental conditions. As an exhausted man is overcome by deep sleep, so comes the sleep of death to man. Death comes so suddenly to many, that it is only with great difficulty that they realise that they have left the material world and entered this world of spirits. Bewildered by the many new and beautiful things that they see around them, they imagine that they are visiting some country or city of the physical world, which they have not seen before. It is only when they have been more fully instructed, and realise that their spiritual body is different from their former material body, that they allow that they have, in fact, been transferred from the material world to the realm of spirits."

Another of the saints, who was present, gave this further answer to my question, "Usually", he said, "at the time of death the body gradually loses its power of feeling. It has no pain, but is simply overcome by a sense of drowsiness. Sometimes in cases of great weakness, or after accident, the spirit departs while the body is still unconscious. Then the spirits of those who have lived without thought of, or preparation for, entering the spiritual world, being thus suddenly transferred into the world of spirits, are extremely bewildered and in a state of great distress at their fate, so, for a considerable period, they have to remain in the lower and darker planes of the intermediate state. The spirits of these lower spheres often greatly harass people in the world. But the only ones that they can injure are those who are like in mind to themselves, who of their own free will open their hearts to entertain them. These evil spirits, by allying themselves with other evil spirits, would do immense harm in the world were it not that God has appointed innumerable angels everywhere for the protection of His people and of His creation, so that His people are always safe in His keeping.

"Evil spirits can injure only those in the world who are like in nature to themselves, and then they can do it only to a limited extent. They can, indeed, trouble the righteous, but not without God's permission. God sometimes does give to Satan and his angels permission to tempt and persecute His people, that they may emerge from the trial stronger and better, as when He allowed Satan to persecute His servant Job. But from such a trial there is gain rather than loss to the believer."

Another of the saints standing by added in reply to my question, "Many whose lives have not been yielded to God, when about to die, seem to become unconscious; but what actually happens is that when they see the hideous and devilish faces of the evil spirits that have come about them, they become speechless and paralysed by fear. On the other hand the dying of a believer is frequently the very opposite of this. He is often extremely happy, for he sees angels and saintly spirits coming to welcome him. Then, too, his loved ones, who have died before, are permitted to attend his death-bed, and to conduct his soul to the spiritual world. On entering the world of spirits he at once feels at home, for not only are his friends about him, but, while in the world he had long been preparing himself for that Home by his trust in God and fellowship with Him."

After that a fourth saint said, "To conduct the souls of men from the world is the work of angels. Usually the Christ reveals Himself in the spiritual world to each one in degrees of glory differing in intensity according to the state of each soul's spiritual development. But in some cases He Himself comes to a death-bed to welcome His servant, and in love dries his tears, and leads him into Paradise. As a child born into the world, finds everything provided for its wants, so does the soul, on entering the spiritual world find all its wants supplied."

CHAPTER III

THE WORLD OF SPIRITS

Once in the course of a conversation the saints gave me this information: "After death the soul of every human being will enter the world of spirits, and every one, according to the stage of his spiritual growth, will dwell with spirits like in mind and in nature to himself, either in the darkness or in the light of glory. We are assured that no one in the physical body has entered into the spiritual world, except Christ and a few saints, whose bodies were transformed into glorious bodies; yet to some it has been granted, that, while still dwelling in the world, they can see the world of spirits, and heaven itself, as in 2 Cor. xii. 2, though they themselves cannot tell whether they enter Paradise in the body or in the spirit."

After this conversation these saints conducted me round and showed me many wonderful things and places.

I saw that from all sides thousands upon thousands of souls were constantly arriving in the world of spirits, and that all were attended by angels. The souls of the good had with them only angels and good spirits, who had conducted them from their death-beds. Evil spirits were not allowed to come near to them, but stood far off and watched. I saw also that there were no good spirits with the souls of the really wicked, but about them were evil spirits, who had come with them from their death-beds, while angels too stood by and prevented the evil spirits from giving free play to the spite of their malicious natures in harassing them. The evil spirits almost immediately led these souls away towards the darkness; for when in the flesh; they had consistently allowed evil spirits to influence them for evil, and had willingly permitted themselves to be enticed to all kinds of wickedness. For the angels in no way interfere with the free will of any soul. I saw there, also, many souls who had lately come into the world of spirits, who were attended by both good and evil spirits, as well as by angels. But before long the radical difference of their lives began to assert itself, and they separated themselves—the good in character towards the good, and the evil towards the evil. Sons of Light

When the souls of men arrive in the world of spirits the good at once separate from the evil. In the world all are mixed together, but it is not so in the spiritual world. I have many times seen that when the spirits of the good—the Sons of Light—enter into the world of spirits they first of all bathe in the impalpable air-like waters of a crystal clear ocean, and in this they find an intense and exhilarating refreshment. Within these miraculous waters they move about as if in open air, neither are they drowned beneath them, nor do the waters wet them, but, wonderfully cleansed and refreshed and fully purified, they enter into the world of glory and light, where they will ever remain in the presence of their dear Lord, and in the fellowship of innumerable saints and angels. Sons of Darkness

How different from these are the souls of those whose lives have been evil. Ill at ease in the company of the Sons of Light, and tormented by the all-revealing light of Glory, they struggle to hide themselves in places where their impure and sin-stained natures will not be seen. From the lowest and darkest part of the world of spirits a black and evil-smelling smoke arises, and in their effort to hide themselves from the light, these Sons of Darkness rush down, and cast themselves headlong into it, and from it their bitter wails of remorse and anguish are heard constantly to arise. But heaven is so arranged that the smoke is not seen, nor are the wails of anguish heard, by the spirits in heaven, unless any of them for some special reason should wish to see the evil plight of those souls in darkness.

Death of a Child

A little child died of pneumonia, and a party of angels came to conduct his soul to the world of spirits. I wish that his mother could have seen that wonderful sight, then, instead of weeping, she would have sung with joy, for the angels take care of the little ones with a care and love that no mother ever could show. I heard one of the angels say to another, "See how this child's mother weeps over this short and temporary separation! In a very few years she will be happy again with her child." Then the angels took the child's soul to that beautiful and light-filled part of heaven, which is set apart for children, where they care for them and teach them in all heavenly wisdom, until gradually the little ones become like the angels.

After some time this child's mother also died, and her child, who had now become like the angels, came with other angels to welcome the soul of his mother. When he said to her, "Mother, do you not know me? I am your son Theodore", the mother's heart was flooded with joy, and when they embraced one another their tears of joy fell like flowers. It was a touching sight! Then as they walked along together he kept on pointing out, and explaining to her, the things around them, and during the time appointed for her stay in the intermediate state, he remained with her, and when the period necessary for instruction in that world was completed he took her with him to the higher sphere where he himself dwelt.

There, on all sides, were wonderful and joyous surroundings, and unnumbered souls of men were there, who in the world had borne all kinds of suffering for the sake of Christ, and in the end had been raised to this glorious place of honour. All around were matchless and exceedingly beautiful mountains, springs, and landscapes, and in the gardens was abundance of all kinds of sweet fruits and beautiful flowers. Everything that heart could desire was there. Then he said to his mother, "In the world, which is the dim reflection of this real world, our dear ones are grieving over us, but, tell me, is this death, or the real life for which every heart yearns?" The mother said, "Son, this is the true life. If I had known in the world the whole truth about heaven, I would never have grieved over your death. What a pity it is those in the world are so blind! In spite of the fact that Christ has explained quite clearly about this state of glory, and that the Gospels again and again tell of this eternal kingdom of the Father, yet, not only ignorant people, but many enlightened believers as well, still remain altogether unaware of its glory. May God grant that all may enter into the abiding joy of this place!"

Death of a Philosopher

The soul of a German philosopher entered into the world of spirits and saw from afar the incomparable glory of the spiritual world and the boundless happiness of its people. He was delighted with what he saw, but his stubborn intellectualism stood in the way of his entering into it and enjoying its happiness. Instead of admitting that it was real, he argued thus with himself, "There is no doubt at all that I see all this, but what proof is there that it has objective existence, and is not some illusion conjured up by my mind? From end to end of all this scene I will apply the tests of logic, philosophy and science, and then only will I be convinced that it has a reality of its own and is no illusion." Then the angels answered him, "It is evident from your speech that your intellectualism has warped your whole nature, for as spiritual and not bodily eyes are needed to see the spiritual world, so spiritual understanding is necessary to comprehend its reality, and not mental exercises in the fundamentals of logic and philosophy. Your science that deals with material facts has been left behind with your physical skull and brain in the world. Here, only that spiritual wisdom is of use which arises out of the fear and love of God." Then said one of the angels to another, "What a pity it is that people forget that precious word of our Lord, 'Except ye be converted, and become as little children, ye shall in no wise enter into the Kingdom of Heaven'" (Matt. xviii. 3). I asked one of the angels what the end of this man would be, and he replied, "If this man's life had been altogether bad, then he would at once have joined the spirits of darkness, but he is not without a moral sense, so for a very long time he will wander blindly round in the dim light of the lower parts of the intermediate state, and keep on bumping his philosophical head, until, tired of his foolishness, he repents. Then he will be ready to receive the necessary instruction from the angels appointed for that purpose, and, when instructed, will be fit to enter into the fuller light of God in the higher sphere."

In one sense the whole of infinite space, filled as it is with the presence of God, Who is Spirit, is a spiritual world. In another sense the world also is a spiritual world, for its inhabitants are spirits clothed with human bodies. But there is yet another world of spirits, which is the temporary dwelling-place of spirits after they leave the body at death. This is an intermediate state—a state between the glory and light of the highest heavens, and the dimness and darkness of the lowest hells. In it are innumerable planes of existence, and the soul is conducted to that plane for which its progress in the world has fitted it. There, angels specially appointed to this work instruct it for a time, that may be long or short, before it goes on to join the society of those spirits—good spirits in the greater light, or evil spirits in the greater darkness—that are like in nature and in mind to itself.

CHAPTER IV

MAN'S HELP AND TEACHING—NOW AND AFTER

Unseen Help

Our relatives and dear ones, and at times the saints as well, often come from the unseen world to help and protect us, but the angels always do. Yet they have never been allowed to make themselves visible to us, except at a few times of very special need. By ways unrecognised by us they influence us towards holy thoughts, and incline us towards God and towards good conduct, and God's Spirit, dwelling in our hearts, completes that work for the perfecting of our spiritual life, which they have been unable to accomplish.

Who is the Greatest?

The greatness of any one does not depend upon his knowledge and position, nor by these alone can any one be great. A man is as great as he can be useful to others, and the usefulness of his life to others depends on his service to them. Hence, in so far as a man can serve others in love, just so far is he great. As the Lord said, "But whosoever will be great among you let him be your servant" (Matt. xx. 26). The joy of all those that dwell in heaven is found in this that they serve one another in love, and thus, fulfilling the object of their lives, they remain for ever in the presence of God.

The Correction of Error

When people earnestly desire to live lives pleasing to God, the readjustment of their views and the renewal of their lives begin in this world. Not only does the Spirit of God teach them directly, but in the secret chamber of their hearts they are helped by communion with the saints, who, unseen by them, are ever at hand to assist them towards the good. But, as many Christian believers, as well as non-Christian seekers after truth, die while still holding false and partial views of truth, their views are corrected in the world of spirits, provided that they are not obstinately welded to their opinions, and are willing to learn, because neither in this world, nor in the next, does God, or any servant of His, force a man to believe anything against his will.

The Manifestation of Christ

I saw in a vision the spirit of an idolater, on reaching the world of spirits, begin at once to search for his god. Then the saints said to him, "There is no god here save the One True God, and Christ, Who is His manifestation." At this the man was a good deal astonished, but being a sincere seeker after truth, he frankly admitted that he had been in error. He eagerly sought to know the correct view of truth, and asked if he might see the Christ. Shortly after this Christ manifested Himself in a dim light to him, and to others who had newly arrived in the world of spirits, because at this stage they could not have endured a full exhibition of His glory, for His glory is so surpassing that even the angels look on Him with difficulty, and cover their faces with their wings (Isaiah vi. 2). When He does reveal Himself to any one He takes into account the particular stage of progress to which that soul has attained, so He appears dimly, or in the fuller light of His glory, that the sight of Him may be endured. So, when these spirits saw Christ in this dim but attractive light, they were filled with a joy and peace which is beyond our power to describe. Bathed in the rays of His life-giving light, and with the waves of His love, which constantly flow out from Him, flowing over them, all their error was washed away. Then with all their hearts they acknowledged Him as the Truth, and found healing, and, bowing in lowly adoration before Him, thanked and praised Him. And the saints who had been appointed for their instruction also rejoiced over them.

A Labourer and a Doubter

Once I saw in a vision a labouring man arrive in the spirit world. He was in great distress, for in all his life he had given no thought to anything but earning his daily bread. He had been too busy to think of God or of spiritual things. At the same time that he had died another had also died, who was a doubter, obstinate in his opinions. Both were ordered to remain for a long period far down in the world of spirits in a place of darkness. In this, being in distress, they began to cry for help. Saints and angels, in love and sympathy, went to instruct them that they might understand how to become members of the Kingdom of Glory and Light. But in spite of their distress, like many other spirits, they preferred to remain on in their dark abode, for sin had so warped their whole character and nature that they doubted everything. They even looked with suspicion on the angels who had come to help them. As I watched I wondered what their end would be, but, when I asked, the only answer I got was from one of the saints, who said, "God may have mercy on them."

We can form an estimate of the depravity of man's perverted nature from this, that, if an evil report about another goes round, even if it is false, a man whose outlook is distorted by sin will at once accept it as true. If, on the other hand, a good and perfectly true report is received, for example that such and such a man is a devout man, who has done this or that work for the glory of God and for the good of his fellows, then, without hesitation, such a hearer will say, "It is all false. So-and-so must have some motive of his own at the back of it all." Should we ask such a man how he knows that the former case is true and the latter false, and what proof he can give, he will have not the slightest proof to put forward. All that we can learn from such an attitude of mind is, that, as his mind is tainted with evil, he believes evil reports because they fit in with his evil nature, and he thinks good reports are lies because they do not fit in with the evil of his heart. By nature a good man's attitude is the opposite of this. He is naturally inclined to doubt an evil report, and to believe a good report, because this attitude best fits in with the goodness of his nature.

Those who in this world pass their lives in opposition to the will of God will have rest of heart neither in this world nor in the world to come; and, on entering the world of spirits, they will feel bewildered and distressed. But those who in this world are conformed to the will of the Lord will be at peace on reaching the next, and will be filled with unspeakable joy, because here is their eternal home, and the kingdom of their Father.

CHAPTER V

THE JUDGMENT OF SINNERS

Many have the idea that if they sin in secret then none will ever know about it, but it is altogether impossible that any sin should remain hidden for ever. At some time or other it will certainly be known, and the sinner will receive the punishment he deserves. Also, goodness and truth can never be hidden. In the end they must triumph, though, for a time, they may not be recognised. The following incidents will throw light on the state of the sinner.

A Good Man and a Thief

Once in a vision, one of the saints recounted this story to me: "Late one night a godly man had to go to a distance to do some necessary work. As he went along he came upon a thief breaking into a shop. He said to him, 'You have no right to take other people's property and to cause them loss. It is a great sin to do so.' The thief answered, 'If you want to get out of this safely, then get out quietly. If you don't there will be trouble for you.' The good man persisted in his efforts, and, when the thief would not listen, he began to shout and raised the neighbours. They rushed out to seize the thief, but, as soon as the good man began to accuse him, the thief retaliated and accused the good man. 'Oh yes,' he said, 'you think this fellow is very religious, but I caught him in the very act of stealing.' As there were no witnesses both were arrested, and locked up together in a room, while a police officer and some of his men hid themselves to listen to their conversation. Then the thief began to laugh at his fellow prisoner. 'Look,' he said, 'haven't I caught you nicely? I told you at first to get out or it would be the worse for you. Now we'll see how your religion is going to save you.' As soon as the officer heard this he opened the door and released the good man with honour and a reward, while he gave the thief a severe beating, and locked him in a prison cell. So, even in this world, there is a degree of judgment between good and bad men, but the full punishment and reward will be given only in the world to come."

Secret Sins

The following was also related to me in a vision. A man in the secret of his own room was committing a sinful act, and he thought that his sin was hidden. One of the saints said, "How I wish that the spiritual eyes of this man had been open at the time, then he would never have dared to commit this sin!" For in that room were a number of angels and saints, as well as some spirits of his dear ones, who had come to help him. All of them were grieved to see his shameful conducts and one of them said, "We came to help him, but now we will have to be witnesses against him at the time of his judgment. He cannot see us, but we all can see him indulging in this sin. Would that this man would repent, and be saved from the punishment to come!"

Wasted Opportunities

Once I saw in the world of spirits a spirit who, with cries of remorse, was rushing about like a madman. An angel said, "In the world this man had many chances of repenting and turning towards God, but whenever his conscience began to trouble him he used to drown its prickings in drink. He wasted all his property, and ruined his family, and in the end committed suicide, and now in the world of spirits he rushes frantically about like a mad dog, and writhes in remorse at the thought of his lost opportunities. We are ready to help him, but his own perverted nature prevents him from repenting, for sin has hardened his heart, though the memory of his sin is always fresh to him. In the world he drank to make himself forget the voice of his conscience, but here there is no possible chance of covering up anything. Now his soul is so naked that he himself, and all the inhabitants of the spiritual world, can see his sinful life. For him, in his sin-hardened state, no other course is possible but that he must hide himself in the darkness with other evil spirits, and so to some extent escape the torture of the light."

A Wicked Man permitted to enter Heaven

Once in my presence a man of evil life entered at death into the world of spirits. When the angels and saints wished to help him he at once began to curse and revile them, and say, "God is altogether unjust. He has prepared heaven for such flattering slaves as you are, and casts the rest of mankind into hell. Yet you call Him Love!" The angels replied, "God certainly is Love. He created men that they might live for ever in happy fellowship with Him, but men by their own obstinacy and by the abuse of their free will have turned their faces away from Him, and have made hell for themselves. God neither casts any one into hell, nor will He ever do so, but man himself, by being entangled in sin, creates hell for himself. God never created any hell."

Just then the exceedingly sweet voice of one of the high angels was heard from above, saying, "God gives permission that this man may be brought into heaven." Eagerly the man stepped forward accompanied by two angels, but, when they reached the door of heaven and saw the holy and light-enveloped place and the glorious and blessed inhabitants that dwell there, he began to feel uneasy. The angels said to him, "See how beautiful a world is this! Go a little farther, and look at the dear Lord sitting on His throne." From the door he looked, and then as the light of the Sun of Righteousness revealed to him the impurity of his sin-defiled life, he started back in an agony of self-loathing, and fled, with such precipitancy, that he did not even stop in the intermediate state of the world of spirits, but like a stone he passed through it, and cast himself headlong into the bottomless pit.

Then the sweet and ravishing voice of the Lord was heard saying, "Look, My dear children, none is forbidden to come here, and no one forbade this man, nor has any one asked him to leave. It was his own impure life that forced him to flee from this holy place, for, 'Except a man be born again he cannot see the kingdom of God'" (John iii. 3).

The Spirit of a Murderer

A man, who some years before had killed a Christian preacher, was bitten by a snake in the jungle, and died. When he entered the world of spirits he saw good and bad spirits all around him, and, because the whole aspect of his soul showed that he was a son of darkness, the evil spirits soon had possession of him, and pushed him along with them down towards the darkness. One of the saints remarked, "He killed a man of God by the poison of his anger, and now he is killed by the poison of a snake. The old Serpent the devil, by means of this man, killed an innocent man. Now by means of another snake, which is like him, he has killed this man, for 'he was a murderer from the beginning'" (John viii. 44).

—and the Spirit of the Man Murdered

As he was being taken away, one from among the good spirits, who had come to help him, said to him, "I have forgiven you with all my heart. Now can I do anything to help you?" The murderer at once recognised him as the same man whom he had killed some years before. Ashamed and smitten with fear he fell down before him, and at once the evil spirits began to clamour loudly, but the angels who were standing at a distance rebuked and silenced them. Then the murderer said to the man whom he had killed, "How I wish that, in the world, I could have seen your unselfish and loving life as I see it now! I regret that through my blindness, and because your real spiritual life was screened by your body, I could not then see the inner beauty of your life. Also by killing you I deprived many of the blessing and benefit that you would have given them. Now I am forever a sinner in God's sight, and fully deserve my punishment. I don't know what I can now do except hide myself in some dark cave, because I cannot bear this light. In it, not only does my own heart make me miserable, but all can see every detail of my sinful life."

To this the man who had been murdered replied, "You should truly repent, and turn to God, for if you do there is hope that the Lamb of God will wash you in His own blood, and give you new life that you may live with us in heaven, and be saved from the torment of hell."

The murderer said in reply, "There is no need for me to confess my sins, for they are open to all. In the world I could hide them, but not here. I want to live with saints like you in heaven, but when I cannot bear the dimness of the self-revealing light in the world of spirits, then what will be my state in the searching brightness and glory of that light-filled place. My greatest hindrance is that, through my sins, my conscience is so dull and hardened that my nature will not incline towards God and repentance. I seem to have no power to repent left in me. Now there is nothing for it, but that I shall be driven out from here for ever. Alas for my unhappy state!" As he said this, fear-stricken, he fell down, and his fellow evil spirits dragged him away into the darkness. Then one of the angels said, "See! there is no need here for any to pronounce a sentence of doom. Of itself the life of any sinner proves him guilty. There is no need to tell him, or to put forward witnesses against him. To a certain extent punishment begins in the heart of every sinner while in the world, but here they feel the full effect of it. And God's arrangement here is such that goats and sheep, that is, sinners and righteous, separate of their own accord. God created man to live in light, in which his spiritual health and joy are made permanent for ever. Therefore no man can be happy in the darkness of hell, nor, because of his sin-perverted life, can he be happy in the light. So wherever a sinner may go he will find himself in hell. How opposite to this is the state of the righteous, who, freed from sin, is in heaven everywhere!"

The Spirit of a Liar

In the world there was a man so addicted to lying that it had become second nature to him. When he died and entered the world of spirits, he tried to lie as usual, but was greatly ashamed because, even before he could speak, his thoughts were known to all. No one can be a hypocrite there, because the thought of no heart can remain hidden. The soul as it leaves the body bears on it the imprint of all its sin, and when it stands in all its nakedness in the light of heaven, then all can see its sin, and its very members become witnesses against it. Nothing can blot out that stain of sin except the blood of Christ.

When this man was in the world he regularly tried to distort right into wrong, and wrong into right, but, after his bodily death, he learned that there never is, and never can be, a possibility of twisting truth into untruth. He who lies injures and deceives no one but himself, so this man by lying had killed the inner perception to truth which he had once possessed. I watched him as, inextricably tangled in his own deceit, he turned his face away from the light from above, and hurried away far down into the darkness, where none could see his filthy love of lying, except those spirits who were like in nature to himself. For Truth always is Truth, and it alone gave this man the sentence on his falseness, and condemned him as a liar.

The Spirit of an Adulterer

I saw an adulterer, who had shortly before arrived in the world of spirits. His tongue was hanging out like a man consumed by thirst, his nostrils were distended, and he beat his arms about as if a kind of fire burned within him. His appearance was so evil and loathsome that I revolted at looking at him. All the accompaniments of luxury and sensuousness had been left behind in the world, and now, like a mad dog, he ran frantically around, and cried, "Curse on this life! There is no death here to put an end to all this pain. And here the spirit cannot die, otherwise, I should again kill myself, as I did with a pistol in the world in order to escape from my troubles there. But this pain is far greater than the pain of the world. What shall I do?" Saying this he ran towards the darkness, where were many other like-minded spirits, and there disappeared.

One of the saints said, "Not only is an evil act sin, but an evil thought, and an evil look is also sin. This sin is not confined only to trafficking with strange women, but excess and animalism in relation to one's wife is also sin. A man and his wife are truly joined together not for sensualism but for mutual help and support, that they with their children may spend their lives in the service of mankind and for the glory of God. But he who departs from this aim in life is guilty of the adulterer's sin."

The Soul of a Robber

A robber died and entered the world of spirits. At first he took no interest in his state or in the spirits about him, but, as his habit was, he at once set about helping himself to the valuables of the place. But he was amazed that in the spirit world the very things seemed to be speaking and accusing him of his unworthy action. His nature was so perverted that he neither knew the true use of these things, nor was he fit to use them rightly. In the world his passions had been so unbridled, that, for the most trifling cause, he, in his anger, had killed or wounded any who had offended him. Now, in the world of spirits, he began to act in the same way. He turned on the spirits who came to instruct him, as if he would have torn them to pieces, as a savage dog will do even in the presence of its master. On this one of the angels said, "If spirits of this kind were not kept down in the darkness of the bottomless pit, then they would cause immense harm wherever they might go. This man's conscience is so dead that, even after he has reached the world of spirits, he fails to recognise that, by murdering and robbing in the world, he has wasted his own spiritual wealth, and destroyed his own spiritual discernment and life. He killed and destroyed others, but in reality he has destroyed himself. God alone knows if this man, and those who are like him, will remain in torment for ages or for ever."

After this the angels appointed to the duty took him, and shut him down in the darkness from which he is not permitted to come out. The state of evildoers in that place is so terrible, and so inexpressibly fierce is their torment, that those who see them tremble at the sight.

Because of the limitations of our worldly speech we can only say this, that wherever the soul of a sinner is, always and in every way, there is nothing but pain that ceases not for a moment. A kind of lightless fire burns for ever and torments these souls, but neither are they altogether consumed, nor does the fire die out. A spirit who was watching what had just happened said, "Who knows but that in the end this may not be a cleansing flame?"

In the dark part of the world of spirits, which is called Hell, there are many grades and planes, and the particular one in which any spirit lives in suffering is dependent on the quantity and character of his sins. It is a fact that God made them all in His own, that is in His Son's image, Who is the image of the Unseen God (Gen. i. 26, 27; Col. i. 15), yet by their connection with sin they have disfigured this image, and have made it unbeautiful and evil. They have, indeed, a kind of spiritual body, but it is exceedingly loathsome and frightful, and if they are not restored by true repentance and the grace of God, then in this fearful form they must remain in torment for ever.

CHAPTER VI

THE STATE OF THE RIGHTEOUS AND THEIR
GLORIOUS END

Heaven, or the Kingdom of God, begins in the lives
of all true believers in this world. Their hearts are always
filled with peace and joy, no matter what persecutions and
troubles they may have to endure; for God, Who is the
source of all peace and life, dwells in them. Death is no
death for them, but a door by which they enter for ever into
their eternal home. Or we may say that though they have
already been born again into their eternal kingdom, yet
when they leave the body, it is for them, not the day of their
death, but their day of birth into the spiritual world, and it
is for them a time of superlative joy, as the following
incidents will make clear.

The Death of a Righteous Man

An angel related to me how a true Christian, who
had wholeheartedly served his Master for thirty years, lay
dying. A few minutes before he died God opened his
spiritual eyes that, even before leaving the body, he might
see the spiritual world, and might tell what he saw to those
about him. He saw that heaven had been opened for him,
and a party of angels and saints was coming out to meet
him, and at the door the Saviour with outstretched hand
was waiting to receive him. As all this broke upon him he
gave such a shout of joy that those at his bedside were
startled. "What a joyful hour it is for me!" he exclaimed. "I
have long been waiting that I might see my Lord and go to
Him. Oh friends ! look at His face all lighted by love, and
see that company of angels that has come for me. What a

glorious place it is! Friends, I am setting out for my real home, do not grieve over my departure, but rejoice!"

One of those present at his bedside said quietly, "His mind is wandering." He heard the low voice and said, "No, it is not. I am quite conscious. I wish you could see this wonderful sight. I am sorry it is hidden from your eyes. Good-bye, we will meet again in the next world." Saying this he closed his eyes, and said, "Lord, I commend my soul into Thy hands," and so fell asleep.

Comforting His Dear Ones

As soon as his soul had left his body the angels took him in their arms, and were about to go off to heaven, but he asked them to delay a few minutes. He looked at his lifeless body, and at his friends, and said to the angels, "I did not know that the spirit after leaving the body could see his own body and his friends. I wish my friends could see me, as well as I can see them, then they would never count me as dead, nor mourn for me as they do." Then he examined his spiritual body and found it beautifully light and delicate, and totally different from his gross material body. On that he began to restrain his wife and children, who were weeping and kissing his cold body. He stretched out his delicate spiritual hands, and began to explain to them, and with great love to press them away from it, but they could neither see him, nor hear his voice, and, as he tried to remove his children from off his body, it seemed as if his hands passed right through their bodies, as if they were air, but they felt nothing at all. Then one of the angels said, "Come, let us take you to your everlasting home. Do not be sorry for them. The Lord Himself, and we also, will comfort them. This separation is but for a few days."

Then in company with the angels he set out for heaven. They had gone forward only a little way when another band of angels met them with cries of "Welcome". Many friends and dear ones, who had died before him, also met him, and on seeing them his joy was further increased. On reaching the gate of heaven the angels and saints stood in silence on either side. He entered, and in the doorway was met by Christ. At once he fell at His feet to worship Him, but the Lord lifted him up, and embraced him, and said, "Well done, good and faithful servant, enter thou into the joy of thy Lord." At that the man's joy was indescribable. From his eyes tears of joy began to flow, and the Lord in great love wiped them away, and to the angels He said, "Take him away to that most glorious mansion that, from the beginning, has been prepared for him."

Now the spirit of this man of God still held the earthly idea that to turn his back on the Lord as he went off with the angels would be a dishonour to Him. He hesitated to do this, but, when at last he turned his face towards his mansion, he was astonished to see that wherever he looked he could see the Lord. For Christ is present in every place, and is seen everywhere by saints and angels. In addition to the Lord, he was delighted to see that on every side there were surroundings that filled him with joy, and that those who are lowest in rank meet without envy those who are higher, and that those whose position is more exalted count themselves fortunate to be able to serve their brethren in lower positions because this is the kingdom of God and of love.

In every part of heaven there are superb gardens, which all the time produce every variety of sweet and luscious fruit, and all kinds of sweet-scented flowers that never fade. In them creatures of every kind give praise to God unceasingly. Birds, beautiful in hue, raise their sweet songs of praise, and such is the sweet singing of angels and saints that on hearing their songs a wonderful sense of rapture is experienced. Wherever one may look there is nothing but scenes of unbounded joy. This, in truth, is the Paradise that God has prepared for those that love Him, where there is no shade of death, nor error, nor sin, nor suffering, but abiding peace and joy.

The Mansions of Heaven

Then I saw this man of God examining his appointed mansion from a great distance, for in heaven all things are spiritual, and the spiritual eye can see through all intervening things, and on to immeasurable distances. Through all the immensity of heaven God's love is manifest, and everywhere in it all kinds of His creatures can be seen praising and thanking Him in an unending state of joy. When this man of God, in company with the angels, arrived at the door of his appointed mansion, he saw written on it in shining letters the word "Welcome", and from the letters themselves "Welcome, Welcome" in audible sound was repeated and repeated again. When he had entered his home, to his surprise he found the Lord there before him. At this his joy was more than we can describe, and he exclaimed, "I left the Lord's presence and came here at His command, but I find that the Lord Himself is here to dwell with me." In the mansion was everything that his imagination could have conceived, and every one was ready to serve him. In the near-by houses saints, like-minded to himself, lived in happy fellowship. For this heavenly house is the kingdom which has been prepared for the saints from the foundation of the world (Matt. xxv. 34), and this is the glorious future that awaits every true follower of Christ.

A proud Minister and a humble Workman

A minister who looked on himself as an exceedingly learned and religious man died at a ripe old age. And without doubt he was a good man. When the angels came to take him to the place appointed for him by the Lord in the world of spirits, they brought him into the intermediate state, and left him there with many other good spirits, who had lately arrived, in charge of those angels who are appointed to instruct good souls, while they themselves went back to usher in another good spirit.

In that intermediate heaven there are grades above grades right up to the higher heavens, and the grade into which any soul is admitted for instruction is determined by the real goodness of his life on earth. When the angels, who had put this minister in his grade, came back conducting in the other soul, for whom they had gone, they brought him up beyond the grade in which the minister was, on their way up to a higher plane. Seeing this the minister in a blustering voice called out, "What right have you to leave me half-way up to that glorious country, while you take this other man away up near to it? Neither in holiness, nor in anything else, am I in any way less than this man, or than you yourselves." The angels replied, "There is no question here of great or small, or of more or less, but a man is put into whatever grade he has merited by his life and faith. You are not quite ready yet for that upper grade, so you will have to remain here for a while and learn some of the things that our fellow-workers are appointed to teach. Then, when the Lord commands us, we will, with great pleasure, take you with us to that higher sphere." He said, "I have been teaching people all my life about the way to reach heaven. What more have I to learn? I know all about it." Then the instructing angels said, "They must go up now, we can't detain them, but we will answer your question. My friend, do not be offended if we speak plainly, for it is for your good. You think you are alone here, but the Lord is also here though you cannot see Him. The pride that you displayed when you said 'I know all about it' prevents you from seeing Him and from going up higher. Humility is the cure for this pride. Practise it and your desire will be granted." After this one of the angels told him, "The man who has just been promoted above you was no learned or famous man. You did not look at him very carefully. He was a member of your own congregation. People hardly knew him at all, for he was an ordinary working man, and had little leisure from his work. But in his workshop many knew him as an industrious and honest worker. His Christian character was recognised by all who came in contact with him. In the war he was called up for service in France. There, one day, as he was helping a wounded comrade, he was struck by a bullet and killed. Though his death was sudden he was ready for it, so he did not have to remain in the intermediate state as long as you will have to do. His promotion depends, not on favouritism, but on his spiritual worthiness. His life of prayer and humility, while he was in the world, prepared him to a great extent for the spiritual world. Now he is rejoicing at having reached his appointed place, and is thanking and praising the Lord, Who, in His mercy, has saved him, and given him eternal life."

Heavenly Life

In heaven no one can ever be a hypocrite, for all can
see the lives of others as they are. The all-revealing light
which flows out from the Christ in Glory makes the wicked
in their remorse try to hide themselves, but it fills the
righteous with the utmost joy to be in the Father's kingdom
of Light. There, their goodness is evident to all, and it ever
increases more and more, for nothing is present that can
hinder their growth, and everything that can sustain them is
there to help them. The degree of goodness reached by the
soul of a righteous man is known by the brightness that
radiates from his whole appearance; for character and
nature show themselves in the form of various glowing
rainbow-like colours of great glory. In heaven there is no
jealousy. All are glad to see the spiritual elevation and
glory of others, and, without any motive of self-seeking,
try, at all times, truly to serve one another. All the
innumerable gifts and blessings of heaven are for the
common use of all. No one out of selfishness ever thinks of
keeping anything for himself, and there is enough of
everything for all.

God, Who is love, is seen in the Person of Jesus
sitting on the throne in the highest heaven. From Him, Who
is the "Sun of Righteousness" and the "Light of the world",
healing and life-giving rays and waves of light and love are
seen flowing out to the uttermost extent of His universe,
and flowing through every saint and angel, and bringing to
whatever they touch vitalising and vivifying power.

There is in heaven neither east nor west, nor north
nor south, but, for each individual soul or angel, Christ's
throne appears as the centre of all things.

There also are found every kind of sweet and
delicious flower and fruit, and many kinds of spiritual food.
While eating them an exquisite flavour and pleasure are

experienced, but after they have been assimilated a delicate scent, which perfumes the air around, exudes from the pores of the body.

In short, the will and desires of all the inhabitants of heaven are fulfilled in God, because in every life God's will is made perfect, so under all conditions, and at every stage of heaven, there is for every one an unchanging experience of wonderful joy. So the end of the righteous is eternal joy and blessedness.

CHAPTER VII

THE AIM AND PURPOSE OF CREATION

A few months ago I was lying alone in my room suffering acutely from an ulcer in my eye. The pain was so great that I could do no other work, so I spent the time in prayer and intercession. One day I had been thus engaged for only a few minutes, when the spiritual world was opened to me, and I found myself surrounded by numbers of angels. Immediately I forgot all my pain, for my whole attention was concentrated on them. I mention below a few of the subjects on which we conversed together.

Names in Heaven

I asked them, "Can you tell me by what names you are known?" One of the angels replied, "Each of us has been given a new name, which none knows except the Lord, and the one who has received it (Rev. ii. 17). All of us here have served the Lord in different lands and in different ages, and there is no need that any should know what our names are. Nor is there any necessity that we should tell our former earthly names. It might be interesting to know them, but what would be the use of it? And then we do not want people to know our names, lest they should imagine us great and give honour to us, instead of to the Lord, Who has so loved us that He has lifted us up out of our fallen state, and has brought us into our eternal home, where we will forever sing praises in His loving fellowship—and this is the object for which He created us."

Seeing God

I asked again, "Do the angels and saints who live in the highest spheres of heaven always look on the face of God? And, if they see Him, in what form and state does He appear?"

One of the saints said, "As the sea is full of water, so is the whole universe filled with God, and every inhabitant of heaven feels His presence about him on every side. When one dives under water above and below and round about there is nothing but water, so in heaven is the presence of God felt. And just as in the water of the sea there are uncounted living creatures, so in the Infinite Being of God His creatures exist. Because He is Infinite, His children, who are finite, can see Him only in the form of Christ. As the Lord Himself has said, "He that hath seen Me hath seen the Father" (John xiv. 9). In this world of spirits the spiritual progress of any one governs the degree to which he is able to know and feel God; and the Christ also reveals His glorious form to each one according to his spiritual enlightment and capacity. If Christ were to appear in the same glorious light to the dwellers of the darkened lower spheres of the spiritual world as he appears to those in the higher planes, then they would not be able to bear it. So He tempers the glory of His manifestation to the state of progress, and to the capacity of each individual soul."

Then another saint added, "God's presence can indeed be felt and enjoyed, but it cannot be expressed in words. As the sweetness of the sweet is enjoyed by tasting, and not by the most graphic descriptive phrasing, so every one in heaven experiences the joy of God's presence, and every one in the spiritual world knows that his experience of God is real, and has no need that any should attempt to help him with a verbal description of it."

Distance in Heaven

I asked, "How far from one another are the various
heavenly spheres of existence? If one cannot go to stay in
other spheres is he permitted to visit them?"

Then one of the saints said, "The place of residence
is appointed for each soul in that plane to which his
spiritual development has fitted him, but for short periods
he can go to visit other spheres. When those of the higher
spheres come down to the lower, a kind of spiritual
covering is given to them, that the glory of their appearance
may not be disconcerting to the inhabitants of the lower
and darker spheres. So when one from a lower sphere goes
to a higher, he also gets a kind of spiritual covering that he
may be able to bear the light and glory of that place."

In heaven distance is never felt by any one, for as
soon as one forms the wish to go to a certain place he at
once finds himself there. Distances are felt only in the
material world. If one wishes to see a saint in another
sphere, either he himself is transported there in a moment
of thought, or at once the distant saint arrives in his
presence.

The Withered Fig Tree

I inquired of them, "Everything is created for some
purpose, but it sometimes appears that that purpose is not
fulfilled; for instance, the purpose of the fig tree was to
produce fruit, but, when the Lord found it fruitless, He
withered it up. Can you enlighten me as to whether its
purpose was fulfilled or not?"

A saint replied, "Undoubtedly its purpose was
fulfilled, and was fulfilled more fully. The Lord of Life
gives life to every creature for a certain specific purpose,

but if that purpose is not fulfilled He has power to take back the life in order to fulfil some higher purpose. Many thousands of God's servants have sacrificed their lives in order to teach and uplift others. By losing their lives for others they have helped them, and thus fulfilled the higher purpose of God. And if it is lawful, and a most noble service, for man, who is higher than fig trees and all other created things, to give his life for other men, then how can it be unjust if a mere tree gives its life for the teaching and warning of an erring nation? So through this fig tree Christ taught this great lesson to the Jews, and to the whole world, that those whose lives are fruitless, and who fail in the purpose for which God created them, will be altogether withered and destroyed."

The facts of history make it abundantly plain to us that the bigoted and narrow Jewish national life of that day was, because of its barrenness, withered away like the fig tree. And in the same way the fruitless lives of others, though outwardly they may appear fruitful, are a cause of deception to others, and will be cursed and destroyed. If any one should object that when the Lord cursed this fig tree, it was not the fruit season, and figs should not have been looked for, then he should reflect that for doing good there is no fixed season, because all seasons and times are equally appointed for good works, and that he himself should make his life fruitful and thus fulfil the purpose for which he was created.

Is Man a Free Agent?

Again I asked, "Would it not have been far better if God had created man and all creation perfect, for then man could neither have committed sin, nor because of sin would there have been so much sorrow and suffering in the world; but now, in a creation made subject to vanity, we have all kinds of suffering to undergo?"

An angel who had come from the highest grades of heaven, and occupied a high position there, replied, "God has not made man like a machine, which would work automatically; nor has He fixed his destiny as in the case of the stars and planets, that may not move out of their appointed course, but He has made man in His own image and likeness, a free agent, possessed of understanding, determination, and power to act independently, hence he is superior to all other created things. Had man not been created a free agent he would not have been able to enjoy God's presence, nor the joy of heaven, for he would have been a mere machine, that moves without knowing or feeling, or like the stars that swing unknowingly through infinite space. But man, being a free agent, is by the constitution of his nature, opposed to this kind of soulless perfection—and a perfection of this kind would really have been imperfection—for such a man would have been a mere slave whose very perfection had compelled him to certain acts, in the doing of which he could have had no enjoyment, because he had no choice of his own. To him there would be no difference between a God and a stone."

Man, and with him all creation, has been subjected to vanity, but not for ever. By his disobedience man has brought himself and all other creatures into all the ills and sufferings of this state of vanity. In this state of spiritual struggle alone can his spiritual powers be fully developed, and only in this struggle can he learn the lesson necessary to his perfection. Therefore, when man at last reaches the state of perfectness of heaven, he will thank God for the sufferings and struggle of the present world, for then he will fully understand that all things work together for good to them that love God (Rom. viii. 28).

The Manifestation of God's Love

Then another of the saints said, "All the inhabitants of heaven know that God is Love, but it had been hidden from all eternity that His love is so wonderful that He would become man to save sinners, and for their cleansing would die on the Cross. He suffered thus that He might save men, and all creation, which is in subjection to vanity. Thus God, in becoming man, has shown His heart to His children, but had any other means been used His infinite love would have remained for ever hidden.

Now the whole creation, with earnest expectation, awaits the manifestation of the sons of God, when they shall be again restored and glorified. But, at present, they and all creation will remain groaning and travailing till this new creation comes to pass. And those also who have been born again groan within themselves, waiting for the redemption of the body; and the time approaches when the whole creation, being obedient to God in all things, will be freed from corruption, and from this vanity for ever. Then will it remain eternally happy in God, and will fulfil in itself the purpose for which it was created. Then God will be all in all" (Rom. viii. 18-23).

. . . . .

The angels also conversed with me about many other matters, but it is impossible to record them, because, not only is there in the world no language, no simile, by which I could express the meaning of those very deep spiritual truths, but also they did not wish me to attempt it, for no one without spiritual experience can understand them, so, in that case, there is the fear that, instead of their being a help, they would be to many a cause of misunderstanding and error. I have, therefore, written only a few of the simplest of the matters talked over, in the hope that from them many may get direction and warning, teaching and comfort.

Also, that time is not far distant when my readers will pass over into the spiritual world, and see these things with their own eyes. But before we leave this world for ever, to go to our eternal home, we must with the support of God's grace, and in the spirit of prayer, carry out with faithfulness our appointed work. Thus shall we fulfil the purpose of our lives, and enter, without any shade of regret, into the eternal joy of the kingdom of our Heavenly Father.

THE END

Made in the USA
San Bernardino, CA
08 April 2018